RESPONSES TO DOROTHY WALTERS' WRITINGS

(Dorothy Walters) is " our wisest and most mature mystical poet."

Andrew Harvey

"Literary Jewels…portals, gateways, invitations into a transcendent sphere… the landscape of LOVE."

Mirabai Starr

"Dorothy's poems speak with the literary brilliance of Rumi, the passion of Mirabai, the humor of Hafiz, and the deep insight of John of the Cross…yet the voice is entirely her own."

Ivan M. Granger

Dorothy Walters is the real thing because for her spiritual experience is primary, and her poetry (like a continuing fountain) comes out of that. She actually has something to say beyond the existential 'me' and the otherwise verbal complexity of poetry that has only 'words' to say. Like all true spiritual and mystical writers, her language is grounded in transparency and grace; and it resonates: her poems are a witness and a transmission. She's part of the perennial stream, and there her work will remain; refreshing weary travellers of all ages now and in the future. I salute her.

Jay Ramsay, author of *Kingdom of the Edge, Out of Time, Places of Truth,* and *Monuments*

Oh wow, my whole body is alive in reading this. It's true! Feels like everything is lit up inside. whoa…

Amanda L.

"Let us be grateful to the people who make us happy; they are the charming gardeners who make our souls blossom."...

Marcel Proust

Dorothy Walters, PhD, is the consummate "charming gardener", who makes her readers' souls expand, blossom,.. and bloom! Her books of prose and poetry on the experiences of spontaneous Kundalini Awakening are transpersonal, intimate, heart-opening, and help all of us, like Kabir, would recommend: "Jump into experience while you are(still) alive!". Her poetry is rapturous; her prose is pure comfort for the experiencer and explorer alike. Dr. Lee Sanella, Swami Muktananda, Ajit Mookerjee, John White, Gopi Krishna, John Woodruffe and Dr. Lawrence Edwards are her literary compadres in descriptions and analysis of kundalini consciousness- - but it is in Dorothy's beloved gifts of ecstatic poems, blogs, caring advice, service to experiencers and explorers, and accounts of her numerous kundalini (subtle and not-so-subtle) encounters which easily award her the status of Divine Feminine Sage.

Jacqueline Arnold,
Founder, Boulder Explorers and Experiencers of the *Sacred (BEES).*

I brought your book to the meditation program I led up in NY on Saturday and people loved it. They also loved your poem from it that is in the recent e-newsletter. I can see from the click stats on the e-mail that people have been going to your blog and to the Amazon listing of your book.

Lawrence Edwards, PhD, LMHC-NY, BCN, CHT
Founder & Director, *OPTIMAL MIND®, Anam Cara*

I love love love these poems. So beautiful and so true! Dorothy Walters' poetry Is intimate, powerful and inspirational, taking the reader on a captivating page turner. If you are undergoing a Kundalini awakening or are on a spiritual journey this courageous and beautifully written book is a gift.

Diane Knoll, D. Min.,
author of *Mysticism & Whales: A Pilgrimage*

Especially during these dark and uncertain times when the very arc of human and planetary destiny stretches us in unimaginable ways and threatens to break the heart and weaken the will, Dorothy's mystical poetry has an urgency and necessity – that of realignment with our Source and the profound love that union sparks. We are reminded by her wisdom and the majestic poetry she generously shares to remember and embody the truth of who we really are. Dorothy lights the way to our divinity and inspires us to offer our unique gifts to the future we are called in love to create together.

Claudia Helade,
Jungian paychotherapist, writer, artist, mystic

Better than hours of meditation, Dorothy Walters' s poetry brings me to the depths of my being and cracks my heart open a bit more each time. This book with these poems is a gift to humanity!

Julie Pogachefsky, J.D, Yoga teacher,
advanced yoga workshops, nature lover, wisdom consultations

YouTube

YouTube video of her at "Dorothy Walters and Andrew Harvey read from her *Some Kiss We Want: Poems Selected and New.*"

"Dorothy Walters and Andrew Harvey: Interview." (Dorothy's story)

"Dorothy Walters and Andrew Harvey: Kundalini" (a conversation on this topic)

"Dorothy Walters and Andrew Harvey Read from New Works" (Andrew reads poems from "Turn Me to Gold"—translations by Andrew from Kabir; Dorothy reads from "The Kundalini Poems)

Batgap Interview (Buddha at the Gas Pump)

The Kundalini Hour (interview and discussion)

The Goddess Speaks

Speaks

POEMS OF ECSTASY AND TRANSFIGURATION

by Dorothy Walters, PhD

THE GODDESS SPEAKS:
POEMS OF ECSTASY AND TRANSFIGURATION
by Dorothy Walters

ISBN-13: 978-1-7352650-4-9

Emergence Education Press
P.O. Box 63767, Philadelphia, PA 19147
www.EmergenceEducation.com

For more information about Dorothy Walters visit:
www.DorothyWalters.com

Dedication

This book is dedicated to our planet,
which is now undergoing struggles to exist
as it goes through the birth canal of a new being,
indeed a mutation of ourselves into our next formulation.

ACKNOWLEDGEMENTS

Many have helped in the creation of this project through their constant
encouragement and support, but in particular I wish to thank the
following for all they have done to help make this book a reality:

Julie Pogachevsky
Dani Pogachevsky
Gail Kinzer
Diane Knoll
My Facebook friends
My invisible helpers from the other side

CONTENTS

PART TWO - AFTER THE ECSTASY

QUESTION

Q. Who among the poets gone am I channeling?
A. Rumi dances in your blood.

Yeats sings in your marrow bone
Some unknown Yogi of yore
turns as you turn,
brings ecstasies that speak.

Dorothy Walters
September 15, 2020

INTRODUCTION

In 1981 (now almost 40 years ago) I experienced virtually spontaneous Kundalini awakening.

My awakening was abrupt, unplanned, and life changing. Through a series of circumstances (the perfect spiritual storm?), I was suddenly transfigured into a new being, one totally infused with ecstasy as I was given new insights, deeper understandings, and glimpses of what the New Human might be.

I had never meditated or done Yoga and knew almost nothing about Kundalini or how to arouse it. Nonetheless, I was literally transfigured in an instant and left to proceed with only my inner guide to lead me ahead on this radically new path. My unfolding then occupied the remaining years of my life, with only the guidance of the "guru within."

Today, if you look up the word 'Kundalini" on the internet, you will receive 25,800,000 results. But then Kundalini was little known in the West. There were no gurus or spiritual teachers in my part of the world (Kansas). Nor were there any Kundalini Yoga centers as are so abundant today. Indeed, yoga itself was for the most part considered to be an esoteric practice associated with the far East, as was meditation or energy healing or other similar pursuits.

Indeed, in 1981, there was no internet (as far as I know) and computers themselves were a novelty for most. There were, however, a few books on this topic, the most important being Gopi Krishna's volume entitled "Kundalini: The Evolutionary Energy in Man." Gopi Krishna (Indian mystic, 1903-1984) felt that Kundalini was the engine for the evolution of humanity to our next stage of development. I agree, after undergoing the many transformations of body, mind, and spirit brought on by my own awakening in a process that continues to this day.

This present book is the distillation into poetry of a forty-year journey into rapture, widened understanding, and research into Kundalini, its nature and implications for us all as the species undergoes universal transfiguration. Andrew Harvey, distinguished international spiritual teacher, urged me in the mid nineties to write poetry and I have now written and published several volumes of mystical verse as well as two books of prose. "The Goddess Speaks" is the latest of these and likely the last, considering that I was 92 at my last birthday and do not know how much longer I will receive these "missives from heaven." They are in fact "channeled" through me, and I am merely the vessel or scribe who writes them down. It has been my blessing to receive these poems from elsewhere, each divinely inspired and coming through quickly as sacred transmissions from the invisible source of all creativity, here thought of as "The Goddess."

May these poems bring you joy and deeper connection with the invisible reality that is guiding us all to a new way of being even as the outer world of human affairs is in chaos and turmoil. Be open to these new frequencies that are arriving into your body as we are all reshaped into a radically transformed version of ourselves as "The New Human."

Namaste and love,

Dorothy Walters

Who is the Goddess?
She is the energy of all that is.
She is Kundalini, yourself discovered at last.

PART I

Lovers

LOVERS

Oh, you lovers, know
that the one you hold in your arms
is not the one you are seeking.

That one is invisible,
unnamable, unknown.

She will come to you
at midnight
when you are sleeping
and kiss you on your brow
or else when the dawn's
first rays wreathe the hills
and mountains in garlands
of scarlet and gold.

She will touch you
in ways you never knew existed.
She will turn you alive.

Then at last
you will know what Love is
as it becomes who you are.

The Cave Of Secrets

There are many passageways
into the Cave of Secrets.

Some find the opening
by howling and flailing about,
hoping for an answer.

Some discover it in quietude,
silence and prayer,
gentle light descending.

Earnest pilgrims wake up one day,
find they are already there,
already know the secrets,
hold them in their hearts,
whisper them to others
in familiar syllables,
unknown tongues.

A Prayer for our Age

Shatter me into fragments
of gold.

Let the gold flow forth
as liquid light
to heal our needy time.

Let showers of gold
gild each of us,
turn us into reflections
of that which we are meant
to be.

THE WILD CARD

(For Jacquie and Ed, my private angels,
who keep me afloat in this sea of chaos and bliss.)

When it happens,
it turns you upside down
and all the coins fall out
of your pockets,
your appointment book
goes blank,
and you are a child of wonder,
everything changed from black and white to brilliant color.

The earth starts spinning
at a different rate,
everyone is you
and you them,
how can anybody stand
so much love?

Your identity card
is in tatters,
your sense of self
lost in rapture,
nothingness your portion,
but you don't care,
are now just
a pulsating particle
in an invisible body
of bliss.

THE CONUNDRUM

You ask how I can speak
of joy, of love,
when so many are suffering
or in pain.

God does not change
as we pass through
our troubles.
"God" (the Goddess) is immutable,
ever fixed,
watching us struggle
with our challenges,
holding us as we transmute
into the thing we really are,
the perfect self,
infinite love,
now and ever,
holy creation,
endless bliss.

God is love/bliss,
and so are we.

When the Beloved Comes

These moments of rapture,
they come suddenly,
unexpectedly.

When they arrive
I answer.
Who am I
to refuse God?

Who am I
to speak
of right and wrong,
good and bad behavior?

Always one within lies in wait
and springs when I
least expect it.

Always I must be open,
ready to receive
the One without a name.

THE FOLLOWER OF MELCHIZEDEK

"Called to be a high priest after the Order of Melchizedek"
- Hebrews, 5:10

I have no robe
nor even a mark
on my forehead.

I have never worn resplendent clothes
and sat on a throne
in front of many adoring followers,
all waiting to be instructed
as to how to live their lives.
I cannot levitate
nor transfer myself
to other places
by desire or teleportation.

I have never even gone
out of my body
or almost died and returned.

Yet I have had experiences
of making love with my
Invisible too tender
to be told.

I have listened to those
who craved some sympathetic being
to hear their stories
and help them on their path.

I have been informed
with sacred truths
by unknown sources
that have guided me to receive reflections,
to unexpected knowings.

I have received visions and revelations,
danced to different music,
swum in a different sea.

I was the outsider,
always alone in my journey,
always striving to fulfill my mission.

I never spoke
of my ecstasy and pain.
Who was there to hear?

BECOMING OTHER

Sometimes it happens
and we mysteriously open
to new revelations,
fresh insights,
unfamiliar experiences.

What does it mean
to speak to the dead,
to travel through portals
that,shut fast for so long,
suddenly swing open
and allow us to see
in a world where
with new eyes, saints' eyes,
all is shining and new,
even the faces of friends,
the trash at the corner?

Or listen to celestial music
or leave our bodies
and gaze in wonder
at ourselves down below?

How can we suddenly
open to universal love,
as if we ourselves
drew the magic card
to take us there, like Alice,
now going down the hidden passage
where all is different,
and we ourselves are transformed
into a refashioned being,

a new formulation
of our old selves?

As if trees began to sing
and messages appeared in the sky
written in the viewer's own language.
Love becomes the universal currency
in a festival of longing,
the invisible made manifest.

POETS' FACES

I look at the poets' faces
and they are beautiful
and wry,
they know things
and how to say them,
they have been there
as witness to small events
and consequential happenings
and taken notes.

I am still struggling
to mold a decent countenance,
each year texture more amorphous,
outlines more uncertain,
as if I did not belong here,
as if it all was a mistake,
and I got delivered
to the wrong planet
and never found my intended
home.

Still, I feel connected
to something
not definable,
something not seen
but felt,
a feather brushing my ear,
a soft breeze
stroking my belly.

Even now
almost no one knows me.
But I am not concerned.
I am hidden and diligent.
Words get whispered
into my ear
and I say them,
And sometimes some people
listen The Goddess

She is the sweetness
that flows through all
and stirs the rocks and trees
to sing.

She is the nectar
of night falling rain,
the pause of the rose
waiting to open.

She is both male
and female,
Shiva and Shakti
locked in eternal embrace.

She is the dancer
in every cell and corpuscle,
the rhythm of the beating heart,
the roar of the waves
pounding the shore.

She is the wind
lifting the birds towards heaven,
the passageway of the
gliding creatures with fins.

She is the myriad stars exploding
as the many worlds emerge
and are swallowed into infinity again.

She has many names,
and each is a veil
masking her true nature.

It is she who embraces
all who call on her,
makes them cry out in joy
and forget all else when she arrives.

You will know her when she comes,
for she will wear your face.

For Kabir

The mystery of words
is this: they convey the power,
even when you do not
understand the meaning.

Some talk about the
unstruck note,
the music of the untouched
lyre,
the unsaid declaration
of love.

And then they give up
and they go whirling about
the house,
ankle bracelets
tinkling,
throat issuing
a sound of joy.

They no longer fret
about meanings
but revel in the moment.

Kabir, my dear one,
you remind us.
I know you.
we have met in a secret place.

LOVE CRIES

"I have been listening to the love songs of Form longing for formless."
-Roche, Lorin. *The Radiance Sutras*

I have been listening
to the cries
of the thousand things
transformed into being.

They sing as a chorus
embedded
in all creation.

They reverberate
throughout the universe
of energy captured into matter.

They vibrate
our veins
into pulsation of delight.

Always they cry out
for union with the beyond
with their song of longing.

They summon us
to the banquet
of unending Love.

SPACE

When God arrives
as rapture in the veins,
we know we are one,
that Source is who we are.

Yet there is vastness
beyond vastness,
space beyond space,
things unseen that nonetheless
exist without challenge.

No one can tell us
truly what is there,
what unseen hand
fashioned such realms
or why.

There is no bridge
to span this immeasurable separation,
no constructed device
to unveil the hidden unknown
we so long to know.

KALI'S DANCE

Kali is dancing
to the rhythm
of the turning cycles
and the drumbeat
deafens our ears.

This is the time
of the darkness,
the place of desolation
and sorrow.

We know of it
through scriptures,
the verses of the prophets
and sages.
We have been warned
and we have turned aside.

Heads are tumbling,
bodies are falling,
the world is melting
before our eyes,
yet our hearts are opening,
the Beloved is embracing us,
our hands are turning
to light.

The Sea Dragon

We did our best not to notice.
Even when the dull roars
from the bottom of the sea
interrupted our conversations
and we had to wait until the
groans and gnashing subside
before going on.

Then we felt the floor
rock a bit
each morning when
we arose.
As if some workman
down below
was riveting things
together
or tearing them apart.

But when the west wall
fell down
of its own accord
we had to admit
that something major
was going on,
a happening that no one
wished to talk about,
an occurrence we could
no longer ignore.
And so we hesitated in dread,
our eyes not meeting,
our tongues swollen
against our teeth,

as we waited
for the monster to appear.

And then when finally he came,
we did not know what to do.
Was it some dark thing
constructed who knows where,
far from our world?
Was it our own shadow selves
coming forth again,
what had been buried
for so long
returning to tell us
that we were
no longer safe,
no longer free
to turn our heads away?

VISHNU'S CHILD

"What thing I truly am I know not clearly:
mysterious, fettered in my mind I wander."
-Rig Veda

Knowing little, I made my way
through forest and rising water
across an unmapped land without a name.

How I longed for the horizontal
mark, to stamp me
as Shiva's own.
Yet I knew
that vertical was my lot,
my calling to be led
by Vishnu, the gentler one,
with intensity I could bear.

Consecrated words were my signposts,
symbols the arrows leading on.
Mostly it was electric current
claiming my body,
my ghost self as love
so long forgotten,
now flowing freely
penetrating each cell and pore
in transcendent union with the divine.

Who sent these massive
infusions of joy
these lovestrokes
from invisible hands,

transfiguring me
into an other,
an unexpected being not encountered before?

What was the purpose of this reconfiguration?
Is this the coming state
of all of us
as we are each one turned to gold?

BLOCH "CONCERTO GROSSO"

Think of being catapulted
into ecstasy, one moment
to the next,
not even a word for it.

No one to tell,
to explain.
No teacher to lead,
no guru,
sympathetic friend.

Day after day,
ecstasy,
no knowledge,
here I am God,
take me,
I am yours.

What is the secret source,
where the hidden meaning,
intended purpose?
Ecstasy its own self,
its self pleasure
and its rewards.

It is our future,
our destiny.
It is who we are
and will become.

THE BEAR

"Suppose you went to sleep and suppose you dreamt that you held a beautiful flower and then suppose that when you awoke you found this beautiful flower in your hand. What then? What would you do?"
(attributed to Samuel Taylor Coleridge)

Somehow I
keep thinking about that bear,
the one with its head stuck in a pail
until some kind soul came along
and freed it,
wondering if we too are just
stumbling about,
heads stuck in something,
going nowhere, really,
supposing
that this darkness
is the only reality,
this place where the only sound
is the clang and bang
when we bump into something
hard and physical,
say a tree or
a boulder in our path,
or detect the roar
of an approaching earthquake,
or a fire breaking through.

What if someone
came along
when we least
expected it

and released us from
this scold's helmet
and the world suddenly
emerged
in Van Gogh colors
against the backdrop
of Mozart or Bach,
and we were surrounded
by angels,
dancing us into bliss—
would you believe
this could happen?

Well, I have news for you.
I know people who
got healed, all at once,
from their lingering pain,
who heard celestial music
right there, on the mountain side,
while they were admiring the view,
or who fell into ecstasy (a state
they had no word for)
one morning when they
woke up.

What if something like this
happened suddenly,
unexpectedly,
to each of us
as we entered
an awareness we could not name,
and when we finally
whispered our secret
into our neighbor's ear
they told us that
something similar
was also happening

to them,
what then?

What would we say?
What would we then believe?

The Mission

"Be a light unto yourself."

-Buddha

The hard part is not knowing
where you are going,
what the distillation
of all those life disturbing events
led to,
why we did any of it
at all.

Was it love we wanted
and kept tracking it
to all its lairs,
each time a lesson learned
and then too soon forgotten?

Was it the sudden opening
to something that seemed
more than mortal,
that flood of bliss
almost more than one
could bear,
for years it went on
and finally subsided,
now ineffable and soft?
What was the source,
why did it happen,
was it from some half remembered
past life?

Who was I then?
Indeed it was a boon,
also a challenge for the times
I lived in,
a life hidden, disguised
in a surface existence.
Did I do enough with that gift,
vibrations raised for a purpose,
a common awakening
into awareness of true self?
Were the poems and reflections
what I was supposed to bring in,
capture in a special vocabulary?

Was it this,
this silence of solitude,
this safety of aloneness,
this being only here,
only with whatever it is
that remains within,
still not aware
where it all leads,
what it meant,
faith that all is well though not revealed?

Her Legacy

(for Mary Oliver)

Her legacy was her poems
and her words were written in gold.

She reminded us of
what we knew
and often had forgotten.

The woods were her
sanctuary, the ponds her sacred font.
She worshipped there
like any true believer,
and blessed all its inhabitants
including frogs and spiders,
bears and foxes,
the airy creatures from the sky.

Her votive candles were the flaming trees at sunset,
her sacred perfume the scent of pines and oaks.
She told us in immaculate language
what we needed to know
about the wilderness without,
the wildness within,
the warm animal of our body
we call soul.

THE HIDDEN POET

Later someone, anyone, may wonder
who she was,
what her thoughts were,
where she lived
and why, alone or
mated.

Some lonely student
may rummage archives,
seek interviews,
old letters and photos
and find in any of these
little trace of the hand
that wrote,
the lost image
in the mirror.

In death
as in life
she was mostly
hidden from the world.
She wrote from
the inner compulsion,
the inescapable urgency
to translate the ineffable
into words,
to tell the unseeing world
how it was
to have been struck
by the lightning of
the unknown,
to have been the bride

of uncommon necessity,
one for whom
the unseen lover
and the verbal expression
were the only visible
constants,
the only things
that mattered.

The Rumi Poems

1. If I Had Known

If I had known
what this journey demanded,
I would never have come here
to this place with no name
or designation.

Oh, well,
let me be honest.
Wild horses
could not have
kept me away.

2. Our Meetings Were In Secret

Our meetings were in secret.
Such things are not to be told.

Yet I keep breaking my vow
of silence,
spreading the news abroad,
cracking the world's heart
wide open.

3. If You Want Me

If you want me
I will lie down
and wait for you
to come.

If you wish to whisper
secrets
into my ear,
I will speak them
for the world to hear.

If you like to say poems,
I will be your scribe,
your dedicated amanuensis,
your tongue of fire.

4. Do You Live In Me?

Do you live in me,
or I in you?
Have we been together
always,
or recently met?
What will happen
if we mate?
What progeny
will we produce?

5. Sometimes I Almost Glimpse You

Sometimes I almost glimpse you
just disappearing around the corner
of my eye.

Mostly you come invisibly,
like a wind ghost
crying in the pines
nearby.

6. I Don't Know

I don't know
what pulled me to you.

Your love magnet
could not be resisted.

Your net of longing
flung so wide,
captured me,
made me your willing slave.

7. This Scandal Between Us
This scandal between us
has been going on for years.

Will it continue
in the other realm?
The place where it all began?

8. Somewhere Out There

Somewhere out there,
is someone
sending signals.

I am the receiver
trying to catch
all the messages,
hoping the static will clear.

9. Rumi, You Rascal

Rumi, you rascal,
I know you are sending
me messages,
too numerous
to count.

O.K., let's be upfront
with all this.

You keep on speaking
as you twirl,
and I
am learning to fly.

THE PASSAGEWAY

To know what I am talking about,
you must tear yourself open,
the way light penetrates a curtain,
turns it into a flourish of illumination.

Then you must lie down.
Become a sky burial
limb parted from limb,
organs torn asunder.

What you have called yours
will no longer apply.
No shred of flesh,
no bone connections
will remain.
The hungry animal of love will find you.

When, finally,
you have become nothing,
the moment will arrive,
you will burst into
a bundle of light,
find yourself in an infinite
field of love,
a new vibration,
shaped finally into what you are.

HOLY WOUNDS

"When the breeze blew from the turret, as I parted his hair,
It wounded my neck with its gentle hand, suspending all my senses."
-Saint John of the Cross

Not at night
but by light of day
You came,
one for whom
I had no name,
yet I knew it was You,
the one I had waited for
so long.

And so you wounded me
with love,
rapture so intense
I had no word
to speak it,
could not say its origin
or end.

Our rendezvous could
not be told,
but in silence
we joined
as if a god descended
to earth
and sought its mortal
counterpart.

And I lay ravished
night and day,
for time uncounted
and now am left to wonder
what that purpose was,
how it still returns,
so many days and years,
rapture unveiling my soul,
taking me into the hidden realms
of my beginning,
my destined end.
The Holy Others

Now I want only
to contemplate the holy ones,
how their lives were shaped
to an intention
as clay is shaped
to mold, permanent
and strong.

How they rose early
to receive the blessing
of the sun,
how at night
they bedded with the stars,
heard the celestial lullabies
soothing them
into sleep.

Teresa in her ecstasy,
heart pierced by
the angelic lance,
John, his neck opened
by a wound of love.

I look for them
even now,
even when the books say
they are gone,
wafted up into a place
that has no name,
living still in our minds,
our yearning hearts.

Unexepected Rapture in a Chair

As always
You arrived
unannounced.

It started in the head
and moved slowly down.

Each tiny pore and opening
filling with love,
so soft,
so subtle,
my hands moving
from a distance,
divine caress.

Rose soothing cheek.
Feather touching self.

Love strokes.
Connection.

Even now.
Even here.

SOMETIMES A WILD GOD

"Sometimes a wild god comes to the table."
-Tom Hirons

He doesn't knock.
He simply appears
in the middle of your
living room.
He wants to dance with you.
He begins to swirl and
you take a turn or two
together.
You feel his breath
like a sweet cloud
upon your neck.
His energy self
begins to flow as frequency
into yours.
Then he wants to
kiss you.

He says, "We have done this before.
Many times in the forest,
by the stream,
while the birds sang
and the swaying branches beat time
overhead.
Sometimes we lay down together,
moss and aspen leaves
for our bed.
Sometimes we spawned new life,
most of whom remained
in our forest retreat.

You have simply forgotten
your beginnings.
Your gadgets and possessions
have blacked out your
memory of the lost times.
The times when you were a god,
when you danced in the forest,
played your flute between the chorus
of echoing stars.

I have come to remind you
who you are,
help you remember
how to dance."

MORNING PRACTICE

Light flows
from crown to soles.

Something moving inside,
"I'm here."
Together stroking the intangibles,
hands caressing the unknowable.

Expansion of the sensed,
not touched.

Place, no place.
Time, no time.

The love field swelling
to the limits of everything,
all included.

PART TWO

After the Ecstasy

AFTER THE ECSTASY

After the ecstasy,
the quiet joy.

After the tumult,
the sweet stillness.

After the knowing,
the irreducible mystery.

After the striving,
the final surrender.

Om Shanti Om

Who am I?

I am a tiny corpuscle in God's breast.

I am an actor in a drama I wrote myself; an imaginary character
performing
before an audience of ghosts.
I am a voice speaking from within a hidden source.

I am an energy of joy dancing before a shaded mirror.
I am a mystery within a mystery, a question that has no answer.

I am a note in a symphony that extends into eternity.

I am a droplet in an ocean of bliss.

SOMEDAY LIGHT

"Someday light will split you open."

-Hafiz

And then who will you be?
Will you remember when you
held the keys
to a secret kingdom
where you were once
ruler and ruled,
and trees rained golden fruit
into your hands,
where the does and the foxes
came to be fed,
and sometimes you were nothing
but light glistening
through magenta clouds at sunrise,
waves bursting on the rocks
at midnight?

When you yourself
were like a great chord
sounding through heaven,
and stars formed your crown
and waves of ecstasy were
your body?

GETTING READY

At twenty, you felt
that all that was needed
was to introduce them
to beauty, which was also truth,
and they would respond
with joy.
They did not listen,
were restless,
eager
to get out for practice
on the field.

At forty,
you knew better,
had found some close
companions,
shared energies
in an intimate way,
then loss unexpected,
unexplained.
What did it mean?

Fifty, expansion,
the Goddess arrived,
ecstasy extreme,
how did this happen?

Often she returned,
no one understood.
something evolving,
world washed and clean,
beloved within as guru.

Now, readying for departure, you look back
at everything
those passionate encounters,
the seasons of the golden branches,
those sweet thrills
all recede.,

I WAS THERE

I was there.
I wore the thread,
carried the mark
on my forehead,
spread my deerskin
in the forest,
performed the ritual dance
where each small gesture
was a secret code.

I fasted the long holy days,
bathed in the sacred river,
chanted the hymns of devotion,
mated with the Other in ecstatic bliss.

Oh, Shiva,
I look and cannot find you.
My life is a river gone dry.
I cry out and hear
only an echo.

All I have left is this small sculpture
and holy longing,
a wave of feeling now and again.
And then this memory,
this stirring,
this yearning to return.

My Destiny

"I have burned my house down."

-Kabir

I, too, have destroyed it all-
myself, my assumed
identity, my face of who I am.

Sometimes I use flame-
sometimes a mirror of trust.
Sometimes a chopping block
to rid myself
of those false claims.

Now I am free
and can choose what
I wish to be—
a bird crying at midnight,
a salmon swimming upstream,
a page in a wisdom book,
a lost continent,
an invisible cell
in the body of God.

I

I am the seeker,
the finder,
the one who has almost turned to gold.

I live where
blossoms of spirit
grow,
in the nooks and crannies
of the soul.

I have many bodies
and many names.

I am the slow dancer
and listen to music
that others do not hear.

Many seek me
and do not find.

I am you.

MAHLER SECOND SYMPHONY

God knows, I have tried.
I swore that this time
I would not surrender,
let each note and reverberation
possess me,
enter and make my body
a sounding board,
ravishment
by vibration.

What is this strange capacity
of resonance
to conquer
and transform?
To make of me
a sensuous echoing
of bliss,
a being transfigured,
self absorbed and
melted
into that which it
is not,
inhabited by another reality,
forgotten self reborn?

I am the princess
taken and won,
the prince claiming
the prize,
the lonely soul
stumbling
into Eden,
lost spirit
home once again.

Sometimes I Long

Dear One,
sometimes I think
it is too hard,
this impalpable love
we share.

Sometimes I want
to hold you in my arms
in your fleshly form,
to share kisses
and all the rest
that earthly lovers do.

I wish to reclaim memories
of when we knew each other
as children,
the things we did
as we learned together,
the ways of a daunting world.

I know, I know
this can never be
on this plane
with its rigid divisions
of seen and unseen,
spirit and matter.

Nevertheless,
at times I long,
I long,
and try to remember.

POETS GONE

Linda Gregg

And here the announcement,
another one gone,
she was among my very favorites,
a great star
hung in the sky
outshining all the lesser lights,
"lines like chiseled marble"
speaking to all who would listen,
now another blank space on the page.

W. S. Merwin

That time he came,
speaking to the students,
reading his polished verses,
his face changing before our eyes
from the delicate elfin features
of a pixie
to the rough visage of
an ancient shaman,
his headdress a buffalo head,
dancer and speaker of oracles,
and then he: "When I was a child
and we played cowboys and Indians
I always wanted to be
the Indian."

Mary Oliver

Everyone's delight,
transformed nature
into transcendence,
that house with her lines
scrawled across the floor,
the framed poem
I hung on the wall
her enigmatic face,
her wry wit,
her fearless embrace
of transfiguration through
union with the sublime,
almost a transgression
to praise,
darling of the soul,
mistress of holy fragments
of the all.

These were my lovelies,
my comforters,
my language masters,
pillars sustaining me
in this world
and portals into the next.

I must bow down,
I must kneel,
I must thank them
and pray.

THE HERETIC

This is a man
who died for God.
I do not know
the manner of his death.
Was he hanged
for telling the truth?
Was he set ablaze
for dancing in the
town plaza?

The others
did not want him
to be free.
He was not like them.
He did not fit into the pattern
they had chosen for themselves, as had
their fathers before them.

After he died
he floated
on the sea of bliss,
a lonely sailboat
drifting into the harbor
of eternal blessings.
The harbor's name
was Peace.

What They Call It

Some call It Father,
Some call It Mother.
Some speak of the Friend
or even the Beloved.

I think of it as the Mystery:
the unutterable, undefinable,
unknown.

Love is what you are seeking.
Let every thought and prayer
be drenched in Love.
Love is the substance
of which you are made
and of which the universe is constructed.
Allow your spirit
to be assailed by Love.

The Alchemists

"Turn me into gold."

-Kabir

They knew the hidden ways
of turning base substance
into gold.

With their alembics
and furnaces,
their formulas and incantations,
they refined the dross away
and sought only
the pure essence of
a new and precious element.

No one must know
their true purpose,
to transmute the incomplete human
into the purified spirit
of the ultimate self.

And so they worked
in secret,
away from the prying eyes
of a threatening authority.

Their goal was much like
ours today—to reconfigure
our base human selves
into something more nearly perfect,
a being more like God.

KABIR AGAIN

Struggling, declaiming,
wrangling over who
is right.

The world is captured
in a net of illusion.

Break through the nets.
Cut the ropes that bind you.
Free yourself
into All That is.

Only then will you truly
turn to gold.

THE MUTANT

First they pounded me,
then they kneaded me,
until I became
a new being.

Now I knew beyond
what I had known before.
I moved a different way,
spoke a different language,
one they did not understand.

The terrible, the beautiful,
both were mine to see.
Visions peopled my mind,
strange music followed me
wherever I went.

Now I lived among strangers
who wore the faces
of those I had loved before
but somehow
were not the same.

I kept my secret
locked within.
Who I was now
I did not reveal
or even know.

Elegy in a Time of Darkness

Does the light fail?
Our leaders betray us,
corruption abounds,
even the faithful are bewildered
and do not know what to do.

We wander restlessly,
seeking for answers.
Forces are unleashed
that we do not comprehend.
We struggle, but wonder
if our efforts are in vain.

Yet, there is even now
a turning,
as when winter gives way
to spring,
and the tulips break through,
as when the fever breaks
and the patient stirs and speaks aloud.

Everywhere on earth
there are reports of an awakening,
stories of such things
that we have never imagined,
happenings hard to believe.

Some hear music from other realms,
others see images of deity
arise before them.
Some speak in reverent tones
with their loved ones

who have gone elsewhere.
Bliss abounds in a field of light
that grows, spreads ever wider.

No one can explain,
account for such mysteries.
We know that it is happening,
orchestrated elsewhere,
destined to occur.

We are grateful,
believe without knowing,
trust the turning,
the unknown source
that leads us to the next level of
we know not where.

WHEN IT'S OVER

"When it's over, I want to say:
all my life I was a bride married to amazement."
                                        -Mary Oliver

And I in turn want to say I was married
to something called mystery.
She never explained herself
or showed her naked face,
but kept her veils securely
fastened over her face
as if she came from a country
whose laws demanded such modesty.

Yet often I felt
her bodiless body
mingle with mine,
her kisses
arrive in unexpected places.

Often I wondered
who she was,
where she came from,
what her purpose.

At times I almost glimpsed
her secret origins.
Finally I no longer questioned
her origin's identity
why we were wedded as one,
but held her close
and silently exulted
in our secret encounters, never told.

AMONG TREES

When I go among trees,
I think I have come home
to myself.

They more or less
smile at me
as I pass,
and rustle their leaves
as if they are sending messages
or else gossiping
with each other.

"See her. She seems
rather nice. We should send vibes,
make her feel welcome."

I smile back
and bask in their love.
Their energies surround me
and lift me forward.
I am happy once again.

When I was young
I used to climb the great cottonwoods
with their floating gauze
past the bodark huddled below
and look out at the world spread all around.

I peered in all directions,
and felt myself at the center
of all that was,
like the omphalos at Delphi

or the peak of Mt. Meru
where the many realms converge
and everywhere
was where I was.

Now it is different.
I am again a child of earth and no longer know
the unbroken sun of all.
But the sweetness flows in the forest.
The life stream circles through.
This shining, this shadow,
both are who I am.

SWIRLING PARTICLES

Now I have reached the age
where everything surrounding
speaks to me.

I see with Van Gogh's eye,
hear notes crashing
in Mozart's ears,
leap onstage with Nureyev,
no riser required.

What does it mean
that the rose breaks open
in my head,
petals burst open
along my spine,
my own curls the vines tangled
on the arbor overhead.

Nothing of me remains,
only this seeing, hearing
instrument of the divine.

Only these tones,
these frequencies
of frozen light,
these vibrations
of arrested matter.

I have no argument
with this arrangement.
I am glad to be God's emissary,
her messenger of creation,

her faithful reporter
of happenings of the universe,
the one she has created
and given us to become,
swirling particles
in the infinite dance.

THE PRISONER

It was dark in the cave.
And silence carved
from darkness.

We were bound there,
tied so that we could
see
neither right nor left,
but only straight ahead,
where the images moved
before us on the wall,
black silhouettes
of people, implements,
moving things.

We watched in fascination,
for these were our reality,
our accepted truths.

Then I escaped
and entered
another world,
a place where light dazzled
and colors blazed
and embodied humans
walked to and fro,
casting shadows as they went.
I saw that we below
were victims of deceit,
mistaking such shadows
for the real,
falsehood for truth.

I returned
to share my happy
news with my still imprisoned
fellows, eager to set them free at last.

But they would have none,
denounced me as a liar,
a charlatan bearing false goods.
And sent me away.

Now I live in this higher realm,
bathed in light and air.
But sometimes I wonder
if this too is a cave of sorts,
if there are yet other places
with other truths,
other realities waiting
to be found,
perhaps an endless procession
of spheres enclosing spheres,
each more radiant,
more filled with beauty and love
than the last.

(Note: Plato wrote a famous allegory in which he described those who sit
in a cave and are deluded by shadows moving on the opposing wall, which
the onlookers mistake for real beings. Actually these are the false images cast
by humans as they come and go in front of the fires outside. This myth thus
depicts the illusions that the many fall prey to, mistaking spurious images and
mundane goals for the priceless treasures of the mind.
This poem suggests that even such realizations are insufficient. Plato, dedicated
to the pursuit of rational discovery, omits the aspects of feeling, of subjective
bliss, of spiritual union with source.
Thus his is a patriarchal (mental) rather than a matriarchal (felt) approach.
And who knows, there may be worlds beyond worlds awaiting discovery even
by our most evolved souls.)

SWIMMERS

*"In the Gilf Kebir plateau in the Sahara side of Egypt there is a cave
containing rock paintings of swimming figures."*
                                                        -Rich Meyers

No one knows what they are doing there.
Why they are swimming in a desert,
where they are going,
why they are attempting the seeming impossible.

Clearly they had something else in mind.
Obviously they were moving
over a landscape
that is no longer there,
ancient times when land was sea
and visa versa.

Thus do our own lives
oscillate
between land and water,
stability and flux,
determination and uncertainty.

So we move forward,
sometimes rising toward the stars,
sometimes falling
into the ditch
where we cling and pray,
chant and hope
until we begin to ascend
once more,
levitation of the soul,
St. Teresa and the Angel,
ourselves transfigured once again.

THE MUSIC WITHIN

Hearing this,
some fall to their knees
and cry "Father!"

Others raise their hands
and know that the Mother
has come.

Some begin to whirl
and cry aloud.
Others weep quietly,
bliss currents too deep to describe.

Whatever it is called
each knows that this
is who they are,
the organ tones
of their being,
the strings and woodwinds
of the soul
at play once again.

The Life Force: Kundalini

"Everything is energy and that's all there is to it."
-Albert Einstein

*"If you want to find the secrets of the universe,
think in terms of energy, frequency and vibration."*
-Nicola Tesla

"Energy is eternal delight."
-William Blake

What I am telling you
is what you already know
but have forgotten.

Did you remember
that you are made
of frozen light
and sound?

That your body
is not a sepulcher of loss
but a temple of desire,
a Taj Mahal of meaning,
an architecture
of discovery?

That you came forth
from the womb of the Mother,
the place of original energy,
the ultimate Source of all?

Even now you vibrate
in holy frequencies,
pulsate in sensuous
rhythms of joy.

Forget about the world
and its invalid claims on you.
Become the sacred vessel,
the quivering instrument of love.

LOVE POWER FOR THOSE
WHO LONG FOR A HUMAN LOVER

The Invisible Lover Speaks:

Of course I love you,
how could I not?
We meet at that place
where movement and language merge,
where sound and body blend
into one saying,
one note,
one being,
one reality.

Do you not know this?
Do you not feel this
as a vibration in your body,
a frequency you long for,
a tone you crave to hear?

The Human Replies:

Let the others
fall into vastness
or mate with the unseen.
I want to put my arms
around you,
feel your palpable self,
your fleshly glory
against my own.

But like air you have
no shape or form,
like light that moves through water
you leave no sign.

Even when you infuse me
with joy, you never show me
your face.

WHEN SHIVA DANCES

When Shiva dances,
the world yearns for light.
When Shakti comes in close embrace
the world unfolds
as light.

Become Shiva,
become Shakti,
let light flow through
your body.

You are the male,
you are the female,
you are both,
bound together
in holy union.

Only when you do this,
when you become both,
will you become love,
all disparates united
in sacred oneness,
supreme manifestation
of all that is.

Eating Tchaikovsky

It was, of course, Tchaikovsky.
His great violin concerto.
Now played by a strong fist
in a child's body,
perhaps from China,
her almond eyes,
her hidden breasts.

I came upon it by chance,
and it was the sweet vibration
that captured me,
features now hard to recall, like
a love session
that was rapture,
but can't be remembered
in detail.

It began in the hands,
traveled upwards
and then awakened the crown,
opening to god's glory
flooding in
from elsewhere,
then down through each chakra
and bodily region,
ending in breath,
exaltation, supreme moment of love.

How powerful she was,
years of practice
preparing for this moment,
this brilliant illumination,

she making love to her
instrument,
and that in turn
making love to me,
each fiber and corpuscle
quivering in bliss,
indefinable love potion.

They never told us
who she was,
nor spoke the name
of the violin
or the man with the baton.
But then it did not matter.

Another initiation
into mystery,
another transfiguration
into the beginning,
nada Brahma,
endless joy.

Brahms' "German Requiem"

Somewhere angels
are circling God's throne.
They are singing sacred hymns as they move.
These do not heed
what is happening on earth-
the trials, the conflicts, the constant griefs-
any more than a star, a moth,
a spark from a flame.
In their world
these do not obtain.
There is only immersion
in what is forever,
sublime, things we know
little about.

Now the horn is sounding
the coming Presence.
The music swells.
The Ultimate approaches.
Time and timelessness
bound together.

Something like exultation.
Anticipation like raw rapture
before the arriving unspeakable,
what we yearn for.

These sounds, these tones
of adulation,
they carry us closer.

Now they are circling again.

These words for which there are no words.

THE ANSWER

You may think
I am someone
who goes around thinking
I know everything
or at least almost everything
but the truth is I know
nothing at all,
not the weeest particle or
iota, grain or crumb.
Not who we are,
where we came from,
what the world
is made of,
the point of it all.

Once a goddess
held me in her arms
and whispered secrets
in my ear.
I soon forgot her words.
They were more like
a feeling
than a thought,
more like rapture
than spoken wisdom.

When they come back
I know
that I am part of something
larger than my imagination
can hold,
something holy, sacred,
ineffable but indisputably real.

I can't
explain all of this
but I will be a dancer
till I die.

MY PORTION

In truth
there was little hope
for someone like me.
I did not know how
to sound the mantras
with the correct vibration.
I could never form
the mudras
into the proper shape.
As for asanas,
my body was too awkward.
So stiff it would
never reach the correc potsture,
obtain the prescribed positain.

I never sought
Enlightenment
nor did I comprehend
its meaning.
I did not even know
how to pronounce
the names of the gods.

I was an innocent
and had no knowledge
of what was required,
what the texts
insisted upon.

Yet one day
the lotus rose
from the waters
and opened
in my head.
Ecstasy was my portion.
After that
my life
was never the same.

The Outsiders

We tend to look
much like the others.
We walk with the same hesitation
or else perhaps vibrant step.
We go to the same
schools,
write on the same topics,
sing in the same choirs.

But sometimes they sense
that we are different,
as if we are aware of something
beyond what the others
command.
They look on us
as odd, strange,
indeed eccentric.

They think we have unusual
hobbies,
follow strange beliefs,
bow to secret gods.

Not until we leave
and our papers explain
do they realize
that we were the other,
the ones from elsewhere
who mingled
unnoticed for so long.

Only then do they understand
the look in our eyes,
the distant gaze or the intent focus,
as if we were listening
to a song
they did not hear.

THE SOUNDING BOARD

Always I was searching for something,
but I did not know what it was.

Then it happened
and rapture
flooded my veins.

It was now too late
to be instructed
into protocols
and practices..

I had only
the teacher within,
guide who led me
breath by breath,
vibration by vibration,
until each pore
and corpuscle
became a vessel of bliss,
channel of ultimate feeling.

How could I pause
for instruction
on the correct manner of proceeding?
Or wait until the texts told me
the correct way to be?

I was now
an instrument of the unknowable,
a sounding board
for God.

PART THREE

The Secret Ecstatic

THE SECRET ECSTATIC

I moved forward
without teacher or text.
I knew nothing of the rules and regulations
laid out in tomes and manuals,
had no one to guide me
from past or recent times.

What I followed
was bliss
coursing through my body.
This lover arrived,
touched every place
in my body,
opened every pore
in sensuous joy.
Even when my head opened
I had no name for it.

When I turned
this way or that
the bliss became supreme.

Finally I lay on the floor,
arms outstretched,
and said, 'Here I am God,
take me,
I am yours."

This One then became
my constant Lover,
and did not rest,
left nothing unawakened.

No one ever explained to me
how this happened
or why.
I followed the path of ecstasy
for the rest of my time,
and wrote no books of analysis,
no tangled explanations.

I was content
to live in the mystery.
I hid from the scholars,
kept my rapture secret
from those who claimed they knew.
What could they offer
but derision and scorn?
How could they deal
with what was not written about,
thus obviously untrue?

The Ecstasy

The ecstasy is beautiful
but it is not the point.
It is indeed the sign
of deep connection
to the all, the god/goddess
making love
inside your body,
the divine outflowing/inflowing
of eternal grace, ineffable cosmic reality.

Yet beyond bliss
there is another
more profound,
more transcendent state
of being.

Silence, stillness,
final receptivity.
Journey into wholeness.
Vastness sustaining all.

Both are ultimate.
Both are who you are.

GOD YOUR LOVER

"Never trust a god who doesn't dance."
Friedrich Nietzsche

No matter what I may have said yesterday,
today I embrace another truth:
Ecstasy is real, the final affirmation,
the holy union and joining of self
as human
and the unseen divine.

How can you describe it?

How can you tell anyone
what it is like
to be invaded, assaulted,
seized and ravished
by something you can neither
see nor describe?

Summon all your courage
and let it have its way
with you,
your subtle and holy body,
your feeling self.

Know that this is
the heavenly lover,
the world suitor,
telling you secrets
of the flesh and spirit,

creator and destroyer,
who seeks to allow you
this brief glimpse,
this minute taste
of the reality
from which you came,
cosmic orgasm,
universal explosion,
now awakening you
through grace,
through hidden alchemy,
into the awareness
that many seek
and often do not find,
who remakes and transfigures your body
every hour of every day,
each tissue and cell,
accept the kiss,
receive the blessing,
do not refuse the Beloved
who is God.

TURNING TO ANGELS

Some are speaking with angels.
Others are growing wings.
And still more
are the mothers of children
who are recalling
when they lived elsewhere,
have strange memories
of other families,
husbands and wives,
when they themselves
looked different,
had different talents.

Who are these young ones,
where are they from?
Where did they learn
what they seem to know?
It is as if
they have been
to a different school,
sung in a different chorus,
and we are doing our best
to understand what they
are telling us,
learning to speak this
unknown language.

TO MY GURU WHO DID NOT COME

(For those who tread alone)

O holy one,
I longed for you.
I wrote countless poems,
said prayers,
yet never saw your face.

You gave me an assignment,
to follow a path that was, like you,
invisible,
trod by few.
You sent overwhelming
love
into my body,
to show me the way.
Often you came,
often we melted together
into one,
how beautiful, this
yab/yum of the soul.

Oh, my guru, my beloved invisible one,
little did I guess,
that you were my unseen guide.

Together we made our way
into the unknown.
You and I, we were wed,
two souls in one body,
secret union.

Oh my holy one,
You are with me always,
even now.

Becoming Buddha

Now you must think of yourself as Buddha.

You are calm, settled, witnessing.

You have been chosen
to be part of this greatest of moments
of human history.

You are now transitioning
into another state of being.

Yes, there is pain and sorrow
involved.
It is hard to relinquish
all you know and have been.

You must be taken apart
in order to be reassembled,
to become Buddha's own child,
the new one.

This is the time for faith.
The time to be the receiver and the witness.

Allow this to happen.

Become Buddha.

Be still.

THE TRUTH

Do not forget
the truth
you have been given.

Your scholarship
was 2,000 years
in the making.

Sages and prophets
have slaved for years
for this knowledge.

Only now
have the books of heaven
been opened
for humanity to grasp
their treasures.

Secrets are being whispered
into your ears
at night.
Do not forget them
when daylight
arrives and the evils
drop once more.

A Twist in the Road

One day there was a twist
or turning in the road
and after that
I was no longer
part of the crowd.
Although to be quite honest
I had never been part
of any crowd or group
or gathering.
Because I always knew
that I was different,
set apart as if
there were something wrong
with me,
a birth defect,
an incapacity that I had
no name for,
that I compensated for
by the knowing itself,
and thus defined myself
as the unfortunate other,
homeless in the sense
of one who has no home,
just a restless discomfort,
never fully assuaged.

Dante said, "Midway in the journey of our life
I found myself lost in a dark wood,"
and thus began his story of his
long journey home,
arrival at the place
where the angels danced,

where the air smelled
of a sweetness
like honey made by
sacred bees,
like perfume manufactured
by the apprentice gods
learning to be holy.
His journey took years (metaphorically),
lifetimes maybe,
but mine took only seconds,
or seemed to make a transition
from one state to the next
in the famous blink of
the famous eye,
and left me stunned,
immersed in rapture
before I had time
to name it or wonder
about it,
I knew only
that I was being overwhelmed
by an unknown force,
commanded by love
to release all remorse
and regret
and simply be
that which was happening
from which I could never return.

And now I was outside
the outsiders,
alien among aliens,
stranger even to that reality
of suffering I had claimed
as my own.

And so I became other,
both witness and alchemical subject,
experiment in progress
and new being in love with
and loved by the invisible,
nameless suitor,
self rediscovered at last.

THE SKEPTIC ENTERS HEAVEN

Even when she arrived
and was filled with love
she didn't believe it.
Some kind of chemical or
magic trick, she was sure.
Something to make you
feel good, like laughing gas
in the dentist's chair,
a substance people ate or inhaled.

And then there was the landscape.
All those luminous blues and greens,
colors she was certain
they had somehow manufactured,
as if she were wearing a special pair
of tinted lenses,
easy to explain.

When they asked her what she
would like,
she wanted a book of reproductions
of famous artists.
They offered her a glimpse
of the originals,
but she refused,
obviously these were phonies.

So they left her to roam
the libraries,
books on every topic,
and she read and read and read,
oblivious to the display

of golden clouds and shimmering gardens
outside,
the celestial music wafting in from somewhere,
safe in her bastion of doubt.

Not This

What I wish to tell you
is that it is not a course,
nor an exercise
of how to breathe your way
to happiness
nor an object you wear
around your neck.
It is not a shirt
with a slogan on it,
nor the ability to name
each center with an
ancient foreign word,
nor a method to turn your body
into a pretzel
or a notion you read
in some bestselling book
with an invitation to ascend.

It is instead an altar with an invitation
to climb up
and let yourself be
dismembered,
every part and particle,
taken and transformed,
sacred fires burning,
sacred hymns chanted,
you the small pile of ashes
left behind,
the ember waiting to be
transformed
into the nothingness
that you are.

SOMEONE TELLS ME

Someone tells me
this image is not Shiva.
Not a god, does not
exist.

Does Michangelo's God
on the ceiling exist?
Did Buddha?
Bodidharma,
whose name I carry within?

Do I exist? Do you?
Am I a phantasm wandering
through the grounds
of an imaginary world?

Am I a creature
invented by myself?

This is what enlightenment
insists upon.
Many are devastated
by this news, don't know
where to turn.
They wish to continue
as they think they are,
not be swallowed by nothingness.

The form does not matter.
We are each real
in an invisible world.
We are each connected

by an unseen thread
to that which endures
and holds us steady
on our way.

When Shiva comes
into your body
you will know
whether he is real.
When delight suffuses
your being,
you will not have questions.

Tell Me

Tell me I am radiant
I will glow.

Tell me I am loving
I will embrace you,
kiss you many times over.

Tell me I am who you are
I will believe you.
You are my sister, brother,
chosen companion and mate.

How could we be separate,
we are one the way
paper is one on both sides,
flower, stem and bloom,
poet and poem.

When You Came to Me

(for all who know what it is to have a heavenly lover)

Heavy with desire
I came to you.

You, the consummate lover,
took me into your unseen arms:
lightning, frequencies seasoned in eternity,
kisses shaped in other realms,
what could I do but relent?

At last I lay on the floor,
arms outstretched,
and prayed for mercy.

But you were no candles
and soft incense lover.
You were there each morning,
in wait at midnight.

When Zeus came to Semele
she turned to dust.

But I bore it all.
Allowed transfomation to occur,
became other than I had been,
now try to help others
on the path.

THE HOLY MAN

(dedicated to Braco, one of the holiest among us)

When I was
the Dalia Lama
and sat upon my thrown,
they came to me
and asked for blessing.
I gave them each a scarf,
and touched their heads,
the silent currents flowing
from my own body
into theirs.

Sometimes they were
startled,
sometimes sad,
and wept, heads bowed,
as they backed away.

What I gave
was love
coming down
in streams
from the hidden realms,
reported but never seen.

I did not choose this life,
this role of god/man,
but it was given me
long before I came
to this world.

Go and heal this place
of woes,
they said.
Give it peace and mercy,
love so strong
it will reek of longing,
turn its face at last
upward to its source.

O, what if I am
the Dalia Lama
come again
to this place of sorrows?
What message
should I bear?
What love
can I now bring?

ONE OR TWO?

Let the pundits dispute this,
cells do not ask,
They just go on being part
of some universe they
do not comprehend,
nor wonder,
am I it,
or am I other?
Yet I continue to do
what I am supposed to do,
don't need instructions
or answers to the ongoing query,
feel the love overflow,
ecstasy is mine.

(Note: "Advaita" refers to nondualism, non-distinction between realities, the oneness of Atman (individual self and Brahman the single universal existence), as in Vedanta, Shaktism and Shaivism.)

THE MESSENGER

Yes, I know,
I volunteered for this assignment.
Instructions were sewn into my spine
so I would know what to do.

I was sent to the middle realm,
the place where things
have substance and heft.
I was given to parents
who were kind
but did not recognize me.
It was difficult
to be a child among others
who were so very different
from who I was.

It took me many years
to understand all this.
Kundalini was the means,
the teacher, the one who
told me my true name,
gave me messages
pointing the way.

I did the best I knew how
to share with the others,
the unawakened ones
yearning to be stirred.
I used poetry, speaking,
books.
I wanted them to know
that they too were composed

of light, of music— their
corpuscles and cells were
singing to them
night and day.

I did not attempt to open them
too abruptly, but encouraged
each one to be inspired
and find their own path,
lotus unfolding.

I had many unseen helpers
guiding me on,
helping me through the
occasional challenges of health,
or when my heart
was so often broken
in this unfamiliar realm.

At first it was very lonely.
I had no real human companions
or mentors, and I did not trust those
who sat on thrones and proclaimed
a single truth.

Finally, I saw great changes
in my world
as authentic teachers arose,
groups banded together
to accomplish essential goals,
new means of communication
emerged.

I will be leaving soon.
All I can offer now
is my blessings,
my wishes for a continuing

smooth transition on earth
as the new species emerges.
Others will carry on
this necessary work.
I will watch with gratitude
from some other place.
It is possible that if I am needed,
I may return.
Difficult as it is,
I like it here
and would in fact accept another assignment.

Something somewhere wanted me to say these words.

Things Not Possible

"I tell you it has taken me all my life
to arrive at the vision of gas lamps as angels . . ."
                                        -Lisel Mueller

I tell you it has taken me all my life
to accept these things
that are not possible
as real.

Only yesterday
a friend was telling me
how after her father died
his photograph appeared
on her computer screen
each morning as she
came down
for her coffee.

And when her mother died
it was she whose picture
came daily.

And when her beloved aunt
died, her likeness came through,
the single image of her among the many
others (family picnics, new babies,
dogs and cats and horses) on the screen.

When I asked my friend
how that could happen,
she said she didn't know

and didn't need to know.
She loved them all
and was happy she got to
greet them so often
even after they
were "gone."

THE ONE

"Atman is Brahma, Brahma is Atman."

-Upanishads

I bow to it
though I do not know
its name.

I kiss its feet,
for it gives me
a blessing.

I clasp it in my arms
though I
cannot see it.

I welcome it
into my body,
for I love its essence of joy.

I and it—
we are one.

SUBTLE YOGA

If anyone would see me
do what I do,
they would see nothing.
Finger movements
so tiny
they cannot be perceived.
Eyeballs moving
left to right.
Hips in minute
rotation.

No sighs,
no touching
of self,
or else often hands,
(palms turned in)
circling at a distance
around the head
or body,
caressing the aura,
the astral body,
oh, what rapture.

I become
this: a shimmering
fountain of
light, of delight,
of joy to revel
in what I am,
what I will become,
of what you are.

I call myself
a yogi,
practitioner
of subtle yoga,
subtle, subtle yoga,
the others don't
know about it,
how our bodies
turn to light.

I don't think it
can be taught.
Make love
with the invisible one.
Follow your bliss.

THE SECRET LOVER

Oh, friends,
here I am in my nineties
and still making love
with the unseen one.

Sometimes in the kitchen,
sometimes at my desk,
it doesn't seem to matter.

Always the nameless
discovers me,
wherever I am.
I know it is that One,
who has been here
many times before.
I recognize this energy
of my familiar love presence.

Always it is like kisses,
here and there,
inside and out,
never touching.

Some call it Krishna
playing his flute
in the distance,
summoning.
I just name it
the One who comes,
never mind the looks
or appellations.

I wonder what I did
before I had this lover
in my life.
I don't know whether
to talk about it
or keep it a secret
from the world.

THIS MAN (PAVAROTTI)

Is this a human
being or an arrival
from some other planet
where music is restrung
to another frequency,
the domain of the sublime,
or perhaps a god or angel singing
through this chosen vessel,
flowing from
the mortal agent
it has partnered with
to let us hear.

And so we surrender
whatever it was
we thought we were
and become just this,
bliss stream from elsewhere,
celestial resonance.

We listen humbly,
transfigured by what we
cannot explain,
carried on its currents
into the infinite
we cannot define.

VIBRATION OF LOVE

*"Once out of nature I will not take my shape
from any natural thing."*

-Yeats

Nor I
but be a sphere of light
to float above this realm
of pain and joy,
a sun with my own center,
a rapture too profound
to say in words,
a sacred trembling,
vibration of Love,
frequency of all that remains,
Soul unleashed at last.

They Talk of Vastness

What do they know of
splendor within,
infinite love that comes
from an unseen source,
touching your body alive,
with joy, with bliss
in your hands,
your cheeks,
your head and body?

Is this not proof
of the divine connection,
is this not the lover
you have always wanted,
telling you,
"Yes, this is who you are,
infinite extension of consummate rapture,
consummation of ecstasy,
now stroked to love
by an invisible hand,
finally opened
to the vibration of the beginning?

THE FAITHFUL LOVER

When I was looking for you
I cried aloud.
When I found you,
I wept for joy.

Now we are one
in quiet wedlock,
you invisible as always,
me patiently waiting.

Occasionally you arrive in full view
once again,
fresh as ever.

That's how I know
you will never leave.

PART FOUR

About Union

ABOUT UNION

Yes, I know about union,
the time when the unknown god/goddess
slips in and you and she
are twinned.

There is majesty in abundance
when certain music strikes the ear
and you no longer know
if sound is arriving from without
or from your own heart.

Always we are sounding boards
for what we cannot name,
something that lives
within, without,
we know not.

WHEN SHE COMES

These moments of rapture,
they come suddenly,
unexpectedly.

When She comes,
I answer.
Who am I
to refuse a god?

Who am I
to speak
of right and wrong,
good and bad behavior?

Always She lies in wait
and springs when I
least expect it.

Always I must be open,
ready to receive
the one without a name.

What the Yogi Said

You ask how I can speak
of joy, of love,
when so many are suffering
or in pain.

God does not change
as we pass through
our troubles.
"God" (the Goddess) is immutable,
ever fixed,
watching us struggle
with our challenges,
holding us as we transmute
into the thing we really are,
the perfect self,
infinite love,
now and ever,
holy creation.

God is love/bliss,
and so are we.

The Faithful Lover

When I was looking for you
I cried aloud.

When I found you,
I wept for joy.

Now we are one
in quiet wedlock,
you invisible as always,
me patiently waiting.

Occasionally you appear once again,
fresh as ever.

That's how I know
you will never leave.

I am a Yogi

Always there is a new experience,
surprise upon surprise,
opening upon opening,
how can I describe it?

I have a name for it.
"Subtle, subtle yoga."
It is not done
on the floor.
It does not involve
twisting and turning
the body into
prescribed positions.

It demands acceptance,
a letting go,
inflow of that which
almost no one
has described,
few experienced.

This morning,
a new level.
Energy that is sweet and soft
and subtle.
Accessed by acutely slow movement…
and concentration.
It does not matter which way
the body movesI
As long it is indescribably
slow,
a movie ramped down

to its lowest pace,
slow motion enacted.

Who saw golden flame
everywhere
and sewed the words
into his coat?
Now this another new and rarest
experience,
unknown frequencies coming in,
preparation for the next stage,
when the physical body
no longer matters,
when we are pure energy,
light bodies of love,
acting in pure bliss,
delicate ecstasy,
a new being.
Every cell and pore
and tendon,
each bone and sinew
and tissue,
all transmuted,
dissolved,
into the new creation.

Ineffable joy.
Bliss of the spirit.

Can you move so slow?
What are these delicate
sensations resonating
through you, everywhere?
Can anyone tell you
what this is?

Turn Me to Gold

"Turn me to gold"

-Kabir

Turn me to gold,
but first make of me
a pile of dust
hugging the sidewalk
where the people
pass by.

A puddle of water
left by the rain,
waiting its turn
to rush into the oblivion
of the drain.

A spiral of light
traced by the Sufi
who danced so recently
just here,
lost in his oneness
with all that is.

When I am ready,
perfectly still,
turn me to gold,
luminous vessel
of the spreading sun.

CONTROL

If you try to control it,
you are like a lion tamer
controlling the beast,
but the beast subdued
is still ready to spring
at unexpected moments.

You will feel proud
of yourself,
gratified that you
are master
of such a jungle
creature.
You can brag and strut,
teach others your method
of being in charge,
but you are never in charge,
really,
for all comes through
in a different dialect,
another language
that only a few can
speak or understand.

Stand on the street corner
and shout "Love"
and see who answers.
Listen to your own
inner voice echoing.
Follow it.
That is the way
students are chosen
in this school.

THE SECRET

If you think
that the Secret
can be said or written
in words,
or given away in
a workshop,
you are like a bear
looking for honey
in a dead tree.

Or a treasure seeker
wandering forth
with the wrong map
and no water.

The Secret speaks itself
at midnight
under a full moon.
But not in words.
The Secret arrives
in your body
when you are least
expecting it.
No rulers or scales
can measure it.
No verses
can capture it.
The Secret
is yours, and yours alone.
You will know it
when it comes.

Some call it bliss.
Others speak of
rapture.
It is more than joy.
It is the way
you communicate
with the Vast Other,
the Source of All.
It is how you know
you are alive.

MOTHER WAKES UP

So I must ask,
what would you do
if, some afternoon,
when you were ironing
or mending your husband's clothes
(do people still mend clothes?
Or do they just throw them away
and buy new ones, everybody seems
to have so much money these days),
or practicing for your church choir
(do people still sing in choirs,
or is everything piped in?)—
well, whatever it is you are doing—
and suddenly, everything gets interrupted
by a strange and wonderful feeling
and finally someone explains to you
that you are having ecstasy,
whatever that is,
you have no idea,
but how you love it as
it makes you feel connected, somehow,
to something much larger, vaster,
more real
than anything you have ever imagined,
only no one knows really
what this is,
where it is coming from,
why it is entering you,
of all people,
like something you may have read about
in a book somewhere
until you put down your iron

or your needle
and surrender to whatever it is,
something soft and sweet
and beautiful
almost like god himself
(or is it herself these days)
coming in
and yes, for a fact,
like god the invisible
making love to you inside
only now you don't really care
who this lost lover is,
you just want more,
and then more,
and then all,
as much as you can take,
even if you burn an image of the iron
on the clothes,
even if the children must go to school
with holes in their sweaters,
even if nothing matters, ever again,
but this, this ineffable feeling
that is more you than anything
you ever felt before.

THOREAU IN HIS CABIN

I knew from early on
that they could not have me.
Thoreau in his cabin,
Aurobindo in his cave—
they were my models,
the goals I yearned to find.

Always I sought to be
who I was.
Not the false images
they held before me,
the lady dressed in fur,
face painted like a savage
ready for war,
shoes unfit to walk.

Books were my refuge,
music my escape.
Trees spoke to me,
flowers sang in my ears.
The stars whispered secrets,
the moon clothed me
in joy.

I had a hidden world,
invisible to the rest.
It was my place of refuge,
shrouded to all but me
in my abiding desire.

THE HIDDEN PATH

Now is the time
to enter
the secret kingdoms,
to receive
the hidden lore.

Not all are prepared
to go here.
They would be quickly
reduced to nothingness,
flash of immolation,
Semele and Zeus.
Most pass by
without knowing,
the entrance not seen.

Once you go here,
you can never return.
What you have seen
cannot be revealed,
for you speak a new language,
paint in colors not known.
You are now
a stranger to yourself,
a being undefined.

Begin the journey
if you dare.
You will drown
many times over,
be consumed in fires
that have no end.

You may not even remember
how you got here,
why you have come.
You will have taken
the only path you could follow
for it was the one
that led you home.
Transforming

I don't know what to say about it,
really.
I just know that I
feel different, breathe different,
know more.

What does it mean
to move your fingers
in imperceptible motions
and send sweet thrills
down to your feet?
How can you circle your hands
near your body
and awaken bliss in each place?
What is ecstasy?
What is bliss?
What is the source
of the great light within?
Who are we
that we are enabled
to receive such blessings?

How is it that each cell,
each molecule and tissue
is turning to its own
essence of gold?
Who are the overseers,

planning and conducting
this metamorphosis?
All they require of us
is openness, a willingness
to receive.
They are doing the rest.
It is going on everywhere.

How can we withstand
such intensities,
these frequencies of love?

(Note: It is said that in ancient India the yogis underwent extreme austerities and purifications so that they would be ready to receive the intense energies that would come to them when they fully awakened.)

The Ascent

There are a thousand ways
to climb this mountain.
Some do it
on hands and knees,
others, like angels, floating
above the path.

Some have lost their way
and sit lovingly
among their vast possessions,
and wonder why they
are unhappy, what they have done wrong.

Many don't care, proclaim there
is no mountain,
for they do not see it
among their numerous estates.

And always there are countless,
also invisible, helpers,
holding out their hands,
helping us to ascend.

Each Morning

Each morning I wake
and think in my mind
about all the things
I must do that day.
The waiting mail
to be answered,
the bills to be paid,
the exercise I swore
I would not put off
any longer.

But first, I think,
I will say hello
to the great and
wonderful beast
that lives in my
living room,
wearing its own
familiar face,
waiting patiently for
my greeting.

And before I know it
I am lost in the world
of whatever,
from Hindu prayers
to Aretha Franklin,
it doesn't seem to
matter,
I am a captive
and gone into trance
and learning
new things.

Did you know
that certain sites
have millions of
followers,
and they are there,
all hoping to grab you,
draw you in
to their special magic,
whether it is
music flowing
in a certain way,
or someone explaining
what you have often
wondered about,
and all are irresistible
and the bills can wait
another day,
and tomorrow
you can go for a walk,
and get the exercise
you need,
for sure.

BODIDHARMA REFLECTS ON HIS LIFE

Frankly, I am tired
of traveling to strange countries,
telling them
what it is they should know,
how speak, what learn.

I brought with me
sacred knowledge,
some say even taught
peculiar techniques.
It was a challenging
assignment,
but it succeeded,
albeit in forms
I had not foreseen.
I became renowned,
honored in ceremony,
written about in books.

Now I wish to be small.
Hidden in a remote frontier area,
parents kind
but unawakened,
myself choosing
aloneness,
books for companions,
no awareness
of what I had been before.
I sought Western wisdom,
not Eastern lore,
passionate relations,
heartbreak, the whole,
a human of my time.

At the end I was infused
with the subtle body
I brought in.
Awakening was swift,
rapture my reward.
Ecstasy was my guide,
my way of reclaiming
who I was.
It wrought transfiguration,
every cell and tendon within.
Again I was called
to be the pilgrim,
the pioneer pointing the way.
Once more I was the lonely missionary.
Again, I spoke my truth,
helped other eyes to open,
found ways to change the world.

(Note: Bodhidharma was a world teacher who is credited with bringing
Buddhism from India to China, where he introduced the art of meditation.
During my initial awakening initiation (internal) I was given his as my "new
name," though at the time I did not know what these syllables meant.)

RAVISHED

They want something tangible.
Something they can see,
touch, bow down to.

They do not hear
the music in the rain,
the secret messages
carried in the wind.

They craft images
in clay.
make figures
out of wood,
disdain the invisible.

They have hierarchies,
build structures to contain,
create rituals and rules,
make judgments
and pronouncements.

When the spine opens,
all other concerns
vanish,
the self is one
with truth,
becomes a living particle
of holy writ,
composed in rapture,
divine infusion,
bliss.

GOD'S MUSIC

They tell me
my poems touch their heart,
speak to them
in the same register
as the great ones,
Rumi, Mary Oliver.

But I am merely
the vessel,
the conduit,
the receiver
of the songs
that God keeps
singing
in my ear.

OUR FACES IMPRINTED

Why does your face look like me?
Or should I ask, why does my face
look like you?

We are not two
but a oneness,
never parted,
ever a single being
no matter how many,
in vastness and love,
our faces imprinted
on every leaf and stone,
each passing cloud.

Because of Who I Am

I have been entrusted
with secrets.
Indeed, I know things
that others
do not know,
cannot know,
and thus think of me
(smiling)
as someone who is somewhat addled,
outside the norm,
off on a limb
that will take me on a ride
to the moon.
They do not listen
when their bodies
tell them things
they need to know.
They cling to the
straight and narrow,
eschew the crooked
and hidden.
When they finally get here
(and they will, this time or
another)
I will welcome them,
hold them in my arms,
wipe away their
tears of joy.

1

ODYSSEUS RETURNS

I, Odysseus,
am returning home
after 20 years away,
war and adventure,
danger and joy.

In the passage through
the straits of Scylla and Charybdis
I had my men
bind me to the mast
so that I could hear
the music of the sirens
and not in madness drive my ship
against the rocks
where certain death awaited.

On Circe's Isle
my men became as pigs
and glutted their fill
until I found a way to
set them free.

Oh, Nausicaa on the shore,
I took whatever innocence
was left from you
and then deserted under cover
of night.

I knew many women,
slew many men,
return home bearing my scars,
my youthful beard
long since turned grey.

Now I return to my ancient land,
my kingdom, my wife no longer a maid,
soon a crone.
They tell me she was faithful,
duped the suitors all,
those who craved my land,
those who lusted just for her,
her ruse fending them off
day after day, year after year,
how can I reclaim
what was never lost,
return to the bed
with one poster still bearing leaves?

My old dog rises,
comes to greet me,
still knows me after
so many years,
Penelope also knows
I am on my way.

She will weep tears,
cling to my lips,
I will be stalwart,
as a warrior must be,
I will hold her,
take her in my arms,
tonight we shall have
the feast of celebration.

I the king
have returned
and many now will seek my place,
there will be combat, death,
I must prepare to defend,
but tonight celebration,

wine, joy,
the master has come home
once more to rule.

(Note: In Homer's great epic "The Iliad," Odysseus, the king of Ithaca, returns home after twenty years of battle and adventure. This poem, however, can also be read as an allegory of the soul's search for its rightful home. After many false starts and detours we ultimately find our way back to who truly we are.)

The T.V. Guru

She has her robe, her mala, her bindi.
She is speaking to a large audience.
Mostly she is telling me
what was imprinted within
so many years ago,
glimpses of eternity.
I have almost none of the implements
that she wears or knows about.
I search blindly for knowledge
once mine, then vanished,
absorbed into the great cosmic field
of eternal knowledge.
I feel for my bindi.
It is not there.
I hold my mala,
something substantial
that remains,
but I do not know its stations.
I ponder that my bindi
is merely a marker,
a reminder of the Great Bindu,
the minuscule center, the atom
from which all derives,
to which all returns in the well spring of creation.
All I have
is memories and words
to comfort me—
like a melody once heard
that clings,
a face once seen
that fades and remains as mystery.

Who were you?
What was I then?
What was the purpose
of our meetings?
Our secret trysts?

The Scrubwoman's Song

I could be a Buddhist
and look wise.
Or I could be a Tantrik
and be a bit wild.
I could be a yogi
and tangle my limbs
like a secret code
that no one else could read.
I listen to an inner music
that none but me
can hear.
I scrub and dip,
scrub and sway,
to this music
that only I can hear.

You and I, My Dear One

Yes, I know,
we are indeed
embedded in mystery.
No one can tell us,
give us the key,
for where, exactly, we are
amidst the billions
of other whirling objects
in the endless skies,
what we are supposed to be
doing here,
what this project
is all about.

Some of us
find distractions,
turn to jobs,
projects,
games and family
to forget about
our questions.
Some invent complex theories,
write books of explanations,
seek confrontation with colleagues so they
can carry on their disagreements
in journals,
the way of the academicians.
Others don't even ask,
don't see a problem.

But You and I, beloved,
we are the dancers.
We move in sweet rhythms
to secret music
like roses, like trees
stroked by wind.

We are always together
guided by frequencies all our own.

THE SLAVE

I am here
to be transfigured,
so go ahead,
knead me, pound me,
shake me upside down.
I don't care
what you do to this being.
It was yours well before
I came to this realm.
You carried it in
your future plans drawer,
then perfected it in earth fashion
once I arrived.
What I see in the mirror now
is what you imagined then,
this body, with all its scars
and imperfections,
the one you designed,
so I will live with it,
claim it for my own.
Just tell me
what to do
and I will follow your desire,
the way a favorite dog
gladly obliges the master
whom he loves.

Always the Mystery

Who awakened me on that fateful day?
Who led me through those jungles of doubt
as I moved forward without guidebook or guide?
Who danced with me
when there was silence everywhere?
Who sent the music
that thrilled my bones, flowed like a prayer
through my body?
Who comes to me, even now,
when my cells and tissues
are transmuted into love?
Who witnessed my longing and joy
when all was knit together
in the place of knowing?
Who speaks with unsaid words
as I listen in silence?

COMMUNION WITH THE VOICE WITHIN

How can I tell you
how it is?

You must build a temple
with bricks made of air.

Travel with no map
or guide.

Drown in a river
each time you come up
to breathe.

Sing music from the
chorus of the silent unstruck sound.

You must embrace and
be embraced
by the invisible cosmic love/ being
from which you came.

You must craft your gift,
share with all,
the symphony playing within.

This "God"

Who is this "God"
that everyone
keeps talking about?

Is he the one
playing the invisible cello
in the corner?
The source of the perfume
that filled my house
the other night?
The bard who composes
the poems
that I write down?

I do not know
his real name
or face,
but he seems to be
at work everywhere.

polished and refined
to take with you
when you go.

NEW MUSIC

This poet has written
a mountain of words.
I read them in vain,
looking for something new.
Friend, truth is a diamond
shining through the garbage dump
of discards.
Look there for what you are seeking.
You do not recognize it
because you know it so well,
you have repeated it
so many times.
It is like the medallion
that you put on each morning
so familiar you have forgotten
what it says.
Be still and listen
to this new music,
What if he lives inside
whoever I am?

EVEN NOW

In the body,
things happen that
I had no name for
and no one to tell me.

What was that strange current
that moved here and there,
now stroking my cheek,
now commanding me to dance?

Oh, sweet one,
you took me to places
that did not exist,
showed me panoramas,
landscapes where I had
never been.

Even now
you sometimes give me kisses
when I sleep.

The Initiation

There was nothing to see.
No words were spoken.
Even afterwards
I could not describe it.
It was as if
you felt
the breath of God
on your face.
As if, at last;
things were no longer
preparation, but realization,
as words such
as holy, sanctified,
final essence
at last had a meaning,
no longer a metaphor
but a silent awareness
blossoming in the blood,
as you as a thin
unseen,
waiting to see what will
become of me
as I wait for the next
alteration to arrive.

The Mutated Sant Arrives Elsewhere

I have burned my body to ash
and the smoke still rises
from that pyre.
I have drowned my being
in sacred water
many times over,
and each time I rose
for breath
I shouted Her Name.
I have walked through
groves and gardens
that spoke to me,
secrets I could never
recall.
Now I am a form made from
dust and light,
molded together as if I belonged,
moving through the world
imperceptible,
unseen,
waiting to see what will
become of me
as I wait for the next
alteration to arrive.

ONCE MORE, TURN ME TO GOLD

(for Kabir)

Every cell,
each bone and covering.
Let me shine
like a golden coin
spinning in the summer sun,
a yellow leaf
that falls to earth
in early
autumn, late spring.
Let me be a beacon for all
yearning to pass this way,
to become pure,
like the alchemist's dream,
the cabalist's desire.
Let me be dipped
in liquid gold,
now luminous,
radiant as the sun,
complete at last.

When the Angel Comes

When the angel comes,
do not send her away.
Do not dismiss her,
hiding your head
and proclaiming,
I know you are unreal,
something conjured up
from my own imagination,
a mythic fragment,
long lost image
of desire,
made to deceive.

Then you will hear music
such as you have never imagined,
it will come from some invisible somewhere,
but you cannot tell whether
a rock or a star.
You will feel something beautiful
unfolding within
as Love invades
your body
and at last you will notice
that the angel wears your face,
is molded of the same substance
as you now are,
a being made of light.

What I Have Come Here to Know

It did not always arrive
in words.
Sometimes it was
just a feeling,
holding the hand
of someone you loved,
or the tumultuous waves
that washed through you
when you were dissolved
totally and knew nothing
but the bliss of the invisible,
come to claim you
as its own.

I could name things:
Mozart lifting you
to a place beyond the supreme moment,
your body trembling
toward a different realm,
too intense to bear—
those leaves stirring within
as they shared their joy
with me, the witness—
those sweet frequencies that rose up
from earth itself
and captured you
at Tara,
holy Ireland's sacred places,
your heart exploding
with unquenchable desire.

And of course
there were the dark opposites:
the betrayals,
the broken promises,
the desertions by the faithful.
All knit together now
into a single ball of truth,
a blend of everything
into a shining perception
of final reality,
how you are now mixed together
as one.

The Evolute

If you wish to transmute,
open yourself to change.
Le the vibrations of transmutation
flow through your being
like a gentle wind caressing a rose
that opens its mouth to rain,
a bud that waits
for the awakening sun.

Yes, you can hear without ears,
see without eyes.
These are done by the invisibles
again and again,
even without your knowing
or recognition.
But if you are wed
to the realm
of the senses,
you will not reach
the kingdom I describe.
You will reject its perfections
for a world more familiar,
and wonder why anyone
would desire to enter
the realm of the immutable—
you will be content to remain
where you are, perishable
as a shadow in moonlight.

You will never know
the world of
formless beyond form,
the permanent after the ephemeral,
the embrace of ultimate bliss,
union with the unseen divine.
You will never find
your cosmic lover,
trembling as the earth shudders,
shaking within as secret love enters,
all in time with the leaf that wavers
now in your chest.

An Unexpected Experience of Bliss

Something amazing happened recently. When I got up I realized that something special (in terms of energy within) was happening. I "accidentally" came upon some baroque music on my computer. Immediately I felt exquisite energy moving in my body when I barely moved my fingers. The vibration was high, beyond anything I have felt before. It was indeed ineffable, though such words as "sublime, exquisite, indescribable" come to mind. I believe that as we go through this universal transfiguration, we are given sips or glimpses of how a totally "recalibrated" being might experience the world. These moments reveal to us how a fully evolved light body might functionin total bliss. Of course the path that leads to this state is arduous and has many challenges. Is this actual mutation of the species? Some think so. I feel grateful to be included in this process and to know others on a similar path.

Note: The above entry describes the exquisite nature of union with the "Beloved Within" from one who has followed this path of divine bliss for 40 years of practice. Such experience is, of course, indescribable but these poems attempt to capture the essence of recurring Kundalini bliss.

AUTHOR'S COMMENT

In 1981, while serving as professor of English and Women's Studies at a mid-western university, Dorothy Walters experienced a sudden and life-changing Kundalini Awakening into full ecstasy. Dorothy knew almost nothing about the mystery called Kundalini. She did not know of another person who had undergone such an experience. In fact, Dorothy did not know anyone who had even heard of Kundalini, a phenomenon then almost unknown in the Western world. There were no spiritual teachers or gurus in the vicinity for Dorothy to access; only a few texts existed on the subject. Dorothy herself knew almost nothing of yoga, meditation – she had no name for what was occurring in her body. There was no internet at the time. Dorothy was thrown back into her own inner resources (her inner teacher) to guide her through this unfolding process, an ongoing phenomenon that continues in various ways to the present day.

In intervening years since 1981, Dorothy has focused her life on Kundalini, exploring its nature, manifestations and its purpose, through books, videos (YouTube and elsewhere), live presentations, and in especial poetry dedicated to Sacred Source. Now in her 90s, Dorothy has produced this most recent book of poems as a distillation of her discoveries from many years of devotion to Kundalini as the "love force" carrying all of us to our next phase of evolution as a new species. Dorothy sees Kundalini as the divine energy currently erupting across the globe, finding expression in many ways as artists, healers, teachers and thinkers release its potent powers through their various work modalities. The "ecstasy" she often refers to is the supreme delight of spiritual union which carries the erotic flavor of spiritual love but is not sexual per se (though traditionally both use the same vocabulary).

The Goddess Speaks takes us through mystical poetry into the deep mysteries now invading our world, showing us the delights and challenges inherent in the spiritual journey. The poems are "word companions" for our own transformation, giving inspiration and encouragement for all who are open to the "Inner Friend" (the "Beloved Within"). This unseen wisdom guide will accompany us and guide us as we together move ahead in a mutual adventure of massive transfiguration.

Suggested Readings on Kundalini

Many people encountering Kundalini for the first time as well as those involved in an ongoing process wonder where to begin their research into this unfamiliar topic. The following list is arranged more or less in the order of difficulty, with the most basic texts presented first.

Tara Springett—Enlightenment Through the Path of Kundalini: A Guide to a Positive Spiritual Awakening and Overcoming Kundalini Syndrome

This book is "written for everybody who wants to learn about the mysterious phenomenon of kundalini and use it to reach the pinnacle of human development—enlightenment. The book is equally written for those who are going through an involuntary awakening..."

This volume contains much valuable information from a therapist who has extensive experience in the field of Kundalini, although I do not agree with her assertion that Kundalini is a certain path to enlightenment (what is?) I also think it can be dangerous to try to trigger it through intent. I am with Gopi Krishna, who felt that the inner guide would bring spontaneous awakening when the student was ready. Of course, one can prepare for the time when that may happen in order to be fully receptive.

Bonnie Greenwell—The Kundalini Guide: A Companion for the Inward Journey (Inward Journey Guides) (Volumes 1 and 2)

Both volumes contain easily accessible information that is especially useful for the beginner on the path.

Gopi Krishna—Enlightenment: The Evolutionary Energy in Man

Gopi Krishna's Kundalini awakening is accepted as the classic account of how Kundalini awakens and operates within the human system. As a result of his experience, he became convinced that Kundalini was the driving force behind universal evolution of conscious. I agree with him, since Kundalini itself seems to bring about radical transformation of the nervous system, the mind, and the spirit. His view is especially persuasive given the current widespread accounts of kundalini awakening reported across the globe. Further, Kundalini appears to be catching, as often one initiate triggers similar reaction in others close to them.

Lawrence Edwards—Awakening Kundalini

"With his unique expertise in modern psychology, neuroscience, meditation training, and spiritual traditions, Lawrence Edwards clarifies for readers the many dimensions of Kundalini awakening, including practices and meditations for recognizing its manifestations and preparing the body and mind to enter its expansive, empowering flow/..." A Jungian therapist, Lawrence is available for phone consults.

Dorothy Walters—Unmasking the Rose

A Record of a Kundalini Initiation Dorothy experienced spontaneous intense Kundalini awakening in 1981 in a setting (Kansas) where she did not know a single person who had even heard of Kundalini. This book offers an "inside view" of what it is like to undergo such awakening in a process that has continued to unfold over many, many years with only the guidance of the "guru within." It is one of the few accounts of the personal journey written in contemporary times. Many find this book useful as a guide for their own experience, even if theirs is merely spiritual transformation as such, in whatever guise. For the author, Kundalini is the manifestation of the "Beloved Within," a presence which brings recurrent experiences of ecstatic union with the divine essence, as well as many challenges along the way as she seeks to balance and integrate these unfamiliar energies. In recent years, she has focused on writing spiritual poetry and reflections on the journey which she publishes as a blog (www. KundaliniSplendor.blogspot.com) as well as printed texts. She takes inquiries at dorothywalters72@gmail.com

El Collie— "Branded by the Spirit"

http://www.kundaliniawakeningsystems1.com/downloads/branded-by-the-spirit_by-el-collie.pdf

El Collie, now deceased, was a pioneer in the area of Kundalini studies. Her early newsletter (called Shared Transformation) brought myriad responses from those willing to share their experiences at a time when Kundalini was seldom spoken of. Her articles on Kundalini, expressed with eloquence and grace, are extremely insightful. Unfortunately, she herself experienced primarily the negative symptoms of Kundalini, and she suffered much pain as a result, with the result that she pays little attention to the blissful aspects of the process. Nonetheless, hers is one of the most fascinating discussions of the many features of the Kundalini process. The first entries on this site are mainly her own earlier autobiography. The later segments (beginning around p. 61) focus more specifically on personal aspects of Kundalini.

Kundalini Rising—from Sounds True:

(anthology from various perspectives—includes Dorothy Walters on the relation of Kundalini and the mystical journey)

Lee Sannella—The Kundalini Experience: Psychosis or Transcendence

Lee Sannella was one of the first to note the resemblance between psychological crisis and Kundalini awakening. Sometimes one is mistaken for the other. This book is of special relevance to all who are counseling those undergoing apparent spiritual awakening.

Evelyn Underhill—Mysticism:

This book is a classic in the field of mystical scholarship. Though Underhill frames her study in terms of Christian belief systems, her presentation applies equally to all mystical traditions and lineages, of whatever disposition. Since Kundalini is itself one of the great mystical journeys, this book is extremely helpful for those Kundalini voyagers pursuing this path. Note: Skip the first section (too academic) and start with Part Two (more relevant).

Dorothy Walters, PhD—Some Kiss We Want:

Poems Selected and New (poems reflecting the experience of Kundalini Awakening)

Made in the USA
Monee, IL
30 December 2020

55995774R00115